Beauty Marks

STACI PEDERSEN

WESTBOW
PRESS®
A DIVISION OF THOMAS NELSON
& ZONDERVAN

WestBow Press books may be ordered through booksellers or by contacting:

WestBow Press
A Division of Thomas Nelson & Zondervan
1663 Liberty Drive
Bloomington, IN 47403
www.westbowpress.com
1 (866) 928-1240

Because of the dynamic nature of the Internet, any web addresses or links contained in this book may have changed since publication and may no longer be valid. The views expressed in this work are solely those of the author and do not necessarily reflect the views of the publisher, and the publisher hereby disclaims any responsibility for them.

This book is a work of non-fiction. Unless otherwise noted, the author and the publisher make no explicit guarantees as to the accuracy of the information contained in this book and in some cases, names of people and places have been altered to protect their privacy.

Scripture quotations marked NLT are taken from the Holy Bible, New Living Translation, Copyright © 1996, 2004, 2015 by Tyndale House Foundation. Used by permission of Tyndale House Publishers, Inc., Carol Stream, Illinois 60188. All rights reserved.

Scripture quotations marked NIV are taken from The Holy Bible, New International Version®, NIV® Copyright © 1973, 1978, 1984, 2011 by Biblica, Inc.® Used by permission. All rights reserved worldwide.

ISBN: 978-1-9736-5508-4 (sc)
ISBN: 978-1-9736-5509-1 (hc)
ISBN: 978-1-9736-5507-7 (e)

Library of Congress Control Number: 2019902489

Print information available on the last page.

WestBow Press rev. date: 03/15/2019

To Ruth, Rebecca,

and every girl and woman

who bears her own beauty marks.

"What treasure waits within your scars."

- *Touch the Sky*, Hillsong United

CONTENTS

FOREWORD

It was such an honor to be asked to write a foreword for Staci Pedersen's book, *Beauty Marks*. This book has such a potent message for so many who have scars, outside and inside, that may or may not be healed yet. Staci overcame her fears and made a bold decision to answer the Holy Spirit's call to pen vulnerability. Through her obedience, her story now has the potential to transform mindsets to realize how the Lord God can cause "scars" to ARISE from their pain, sorrow, and embarrassment and become "BEAUTY MARKS" of victory, triumph, and testimony unto the praise, honor and glory of our Lord Jesus Christ. She testifies boldly that she is not a victim but an overcomer.

Staci has a committed willingness in her personal faith walk that energizes her to yield her life to the LORD for His grace to do the impossible, which is not limited just to writing. For example, she ran her first 26.2-mile marathon in 2017. She had only trained running up to 20 miles which did ignite some fear in believing she could complete the distance. However, she chose to trust in the God who does impossible things and was able to successfully run without stopping, finishing with a 10:49 average per mile. She intentionally decided to activate her faith, rejecting fear and chose to believe that if she tried to run the marathon, God would grant her the power, strength, and might to make it across the finish line. Her running shirt which said "Running on Faith" became the reality!!

As a college student, she was inspired to establish an organization called, With All Her Might, whose purpose was to "create a community for women with a mission to encourage, strengthen, and inspire every woman who desires to actively, fearlessly, and passionately pursue her God-given calling in life, love, and dreams." She had no real income; however, the lack of funds did not grip her in fear and prevent her in moving the vision forward. She invited friends to come to her apartment and share the truth of their struggles in their lives and experience encouragement through community. She also started a blog, "Confessions of a Broken Heart", and would write what the Lord inspired her to, speaking life and truth to women. Once again, the fear of the how, what, when and where were overcome by her faith in believing that what God had laid on her heart to do could become a reality because of HIM!!!

After her accident, the LORD opened wondrous doors of opportunity for Staci to be His messenger for With All Her Might. One particular door that opened was to the country of Uganda. Staci's visits to this country have filled her heart with an incredible, divine love for the people. She worked with Impact Ministries Uganda which has an orphanage and school. Proceeds from *Beauty Marks* will be used to create a means of support to aid meeting the needs of friends, sisters, and young women growing up at the orphanage who will follow them.

May the Lord Jesus richly and abundantly bless *Beauty Marks* with His increase to accomplish everything He has planned and purposed for it. With Staci's example, may the Lord use her life's story as a witness of His grace that is greater than ALL our fears.

To YOU, LORD, be ALL the GLORY!!!

Shannon Stewart

Season One Runner-Up

America's Next Top Model

ACKNOWLEDGMENTS

Were it not for those closest to me, *Beauty Marks* may have never been. To my parents, "the house that built me", who gave me a solid foundation and helped to inspire a dreamer's heart in me. Throughout my life, you have both been my continuous support and anchor, even through all my "crazy" plans and "what is she doing now" moments. Mom, my friend, and dad, my number one fan, I am forever grateful for the way you raised me, your unconditional love, and from a young age pointing me to God and His mission that instilled in me a passion to love Jesus and love people.

To Evan, for your unconditional love, deep friendship, and constant encouragement that helped me push through all those times I doubted myself, for reading and re-reading my drafts and edits, and deeming me your "favorite writer". And because, through you, I have seen God bring 1 John 4:18-19 to life.

To my dear friends I call sisters, Stacey, Sandra, Emily and Krizia, whom over the years have been my support system, and especially now during the process of writing this book. Thank you, girls, for being there for me, believing in my dream to write *Beauty Marks*, for being sounding boards to bounce my ideas and plans around, and believing in God's dreams for me and With All Her Might.

To Alyssa, your friendship and presence in my life was meaningful in so many ways throughout the healing process. We were the only ones that truly knew what the other was going through, and if it had to happen, I'm glad I went through it with you.

To the Okabe family, for welcoming me to Uganda, allowing me the privilege of working with the ministry, giving me the freedom to use my gifts, and leaving God the space to do what He desired during my visits there. May there be many more trips to come.

To my sisters in Uganda, for opening your hearts and your homes to me, and for giving me the honor to hear your stories and share in your lives.

Last and most importantly, to my God. For His unconditional love, grace, redemption, and beauty displayed throughout the entirety of my life. I am spoken for, and I am, forever, Yours.

PREFACE

There is a restlessness I get when I'm not doing something I know I should be. Writing this book has been in my heart for the last five years, but for as much as I love to write, *Beauty Marks* is a life story I have not written until now. I believed one day I would, and perhaps there would be a greater purpose than in just writing it for myself, I just didn't know when that would be. When fear would creep in, I would try to imagine a world in which it was never written. The pain I felt in my heart to even think of not following through with something I knew I must do, something that could have the potential to touch others and be impactful in their lives, I couldn't stand the thought. The risk of being vulnerable was worth it over a lifetime of denying a God-given calling.

Fearlessness is an attribute I would always hope to be credited as having, but for so long, part of me has been scared to write this, scared to expose and share my own hurt, fearful of speaking out about something so personal to which others may not relate to, or worse, cast aside as worthless. But my purpose is my resolve.

"This does not define me."

After my accident, I declared those words over and over again to remind myself that an occurrence in my life didn't dictate my life, only to the degree which I allowed it, and I was not going to allow life circumstances to change me or my destiny for the worse. Instead, I asked God to give me the faith to believe that this would be one of those moments where there would be "beauty for ashes", and my story would be a testament of faith, courage, grace, and redemption.

I spent a great amount of time discerning how to write this book and the extent of details to include. My first draft contained a heavily detailed description of that night. However, while editing, I felt that most details really weren't necessary to tell my story and still keep its intent, authenticity and purpose.

Vulnerability is a humbling, yet beautiful thing. Being vulnerable while writing this meant sharing my scars with the world, knowing God can use them to change the world. My focus of this account is not what happened that night, but instead, the outcome of it. It's about the process of going through adversity, learning to overcome those things that seem too impossible in the moment, and allowing God to work through them to lead you to a higher calling and greater destiny. This book is a witness to God's hand in our lives and how He redeems and brings beauty to our scars.

This is *Beauty Marks*.

INTRODUCTION

Over the last decade I have named each new year based on what I believe God is asking me to activate in my life that coming year and 2013 was fittingly, my Year of Fearlessness, though I had no idea what would come my way to test that virtue.

As a recent college graduate and having recently moved to Los Angeles for the start of a hopeful career in the nonprofit sector, I was excited to make my new life in the City of Angels count. The story behind making this transition, I knew, was orchestrated by none other than God, and I believed that I was exactly where He wanted me at all of twenty-three years old.

Becoming acquainted with my new life, those first months were pivotal for the direction I was deciding to take with my future. And during a time where I needed God, I found Him in the most obscure and unwanted of circumstances, but His presence was undeniable.

How amazing it is that God uses these types of occurrences, however undesirable, to bring beauty to the world. If we knew the extent of His goodness and the power it has to cover and redeem what has been blemished, perhaps we really wouldn't be so afraid of bad things happening.

Beauty Mark (n.): Physical evidence of a healed wound that represents a greater story being told; God's beauty, grace, and redemption in the scars we bear.

I

When the World Grows Dark

"Mountain high or valley low, I sing
out and remind my soul,
I am Yours, I am forever Yours."

- *Love Came Down*, Kari Jobe

April 12th, 2013. It was supposed to be an uneventful night. I was about to hang out with a friend I hadn't seen in years, but I wasn't planning on anything crazy happening. We made it up as we went. Mine and Alyssa's night consisted of going out to dinner, doing a little shopping, then picking up dessert and a rental movie to watch back at my apartment. Nothing crazy.

When I look back play-by-play of our night, so much of it was so random. Even down to our timing and how that all factored in. It seems as if none of it made sense yet was still perfectly timed out to lead up to it. The last ten minutes alone before it happened played out so meticulously to bring us to where we were at in that precise moment in time.

Around 10:00pm we arrived to my apartment, except I had street parking and it was a Friday night. Living in Sherman Oaks, a suburb of Los Angeles, and being right next to the galleria meant it was busy; it took us almost ten minutes just to find parking, and it wasn't even good parking. Getting out of the car, we walked the distance down the street to the crosswalk that would lead across the street to my apartment complex. Still a way off from the crosswalk, I saw the light would be turning green soon and realized that if I didn't sprint a little to it and push the walk button, we'd have to wait another light.

I wasn't in a hurry, I just didn't think twice about doing it. I ran the short distance to the light and pushed the walk button just in time. The light turned green almost instantly,

the walk sign went up, and when Alyssa caught up to me a few seconds later, we started our way across the street. As we were walking, we were also talking. Alyssa was closer to the intersection and facing my direction, away from it, and I was on her left side, facing the intersection occasionally when looking toward her as we talked.

Almost three-quarters of the way across the street I noticed in my peripheral vision, headlights from the intersection coming our way. We weren't walking slow, so my first thought was one of annoyance: how unbelievably rude of a driver that they couldn't wait for us to fully cross the street before starting to turn left? A second later, when I realized the headlights were getting closer and weren't stopping, I turned my head to see fully what was going on while my brain also began to process what was about to happen. Facing me, Alyssa had no clue what was coming. In the milliseconds I had to warn her, I wanted to scream at her to move or push her out of the way, but there was just no time.

When my mind wanders back to that moment, I still have feelings of disbelief and am a little awe-struck. I remember everything leading up to being hit, but I don't remember actually being hit or the impact. My mind only knows and remembers of that split-second of coming to the realization of what was about to happen and wanting to warn Alyssa. The next thing I remember is I woke up lying on the street. I can only assume it was the force of being hit by an SUV

that caused me to blackout. And honestly, I see the haziness of the moment as a gift from God.

I understand that when traumatic things happen to people, it is a natural response to block them from one's memory. For me, there was never a moment from the point of waking up from being hit, to this day, that I have ever remembered the actual impact of being hit. I see it as a gift from God because even though I cannot recall details, I know it was horrific. I do believe God was with me and was specifically protecting me from not having to relive that moment of trauma for the rest of my life.

In the chaos that followed, Alyssa and I were surrounded by concerned witnesses, one of them being the driver of the SUV, comforting and helping us until a fire truck and ambulance came. Although it is one of the hardest things I have ever experienced in my life, in those moments I knew, even with physical damage done and injuries to tend to, that both Alyssa and I would be OK. I thank God for that.

After spending a few hours at the hospital being checked out and taken care of, we were both cleared to leave and in the early hours of the morning, Alyssa and I were able to go back to my apartment. By that time, my parents had driven out from my hometown two hours away to spend the night with us. At the hospital my wounds had been cleaned, but I still looked a wreck and was finally able to shower. I used that shower to wash the night away.

Based on our injuries and how we landed from the

impact, Alyssa and I could only assume the SUV had struck me and clipped her. Though neither of our injuries were life-threatening, they were hard to accept nonetheless. She had been hit in the back of her head which required several staples that night and multiple neurologist appointments in the months to come. My overall injuries included having a couple teeth knocked out, multiple fractures behind my nose, a busted lip, heavily bruised and bloodied feet from wearing sandals, multiple cuts and abrasions, and a fractured wrist.

Because of the extent of my injuries, I needed help from my mom just to bathe, let alone do normal every day activities no one thinks twice about asking help for. In the first couple weeks after the accident, I went back to my hometown and she became my caretaker. If you had seen me that first week, you would have thought I had been in a bad fight and had obviously lost.

Peace in the Moment

As I write about that night, I don't want to detail solely on the upsetting parts. I still saw God in the midst of the tragic. I felt His peace and remembered the promise of His presence with me. I knew He was with me and Alyssa and that He would take care of us.

After initially being hit, Alyssa and I made our way to the sidewalk and sat down on the curb, where we were eventually met with a crowd of people wanting to help.

There are significant people who stand out in the aftermath that were a blessing. Though I don't have names or even remember faces, I'm thankful for their care and support in my time of need.

I'll always remember one gentleman who approached me with a roll of toilet paper, of all things, that we used to stop the bleeding until the first responders came. Because of my busted lip and teeth being knocked out, there was a significant amount of blood coming from my mouth. As we waited for help, he continued to hand me wads of toilet paper to replace the used ones. God bless him.

One thing I am extremely grateful for, is the woman who hit us not only stopped and waited with us, but was also concerned for our well-being. From the moment she got out of her car, she, herself was in shock of what had happened and continued sincerely apologizing, saying she hadn't seen us. It has always been in my nature to faint easily at the sight of excessive blood, so when it got to the point where I thought I might, I had to lay back on the sidewalk. As I did, the driver bent over, held my face in her hands, and looking at me, apologized again. She acted like a mother. Later, I found out not only was she, but her teenage daughter and daughter's friends had been in the car with her.

When the first responders came, they initially assessed us at the scene. Alyssa was then taken away first and next I was put into an ambulance. While being checked out more thoroughly before we headed to the hospital, the EMT was

asking me to move different parts of my body to evaluate my injuries. There was a trainee with him learning in real time and at one point I was asked from a scale of one to ten the pain level I was experiencing. In reality, I was experiencing the most pain I had ever felt in my life but I didn't want to be dramatic. I wanted to say ten but being reasonable I said I was only at a level six. The EMT used this as a teaching lesson for his trainee. He said that what I was experiencing could very well be a level six to me, but that my pain was subjective. He continued and said that as medical professionals they had to assess my injuries objectively, and he concluded that with my injuries and status, I was probably only at a level three.

In one of the worst moments of my life, I had to laugh at the difference of our prognoses and laughed even more when I realized how ridiculous I must look. Though by this point I think my wadded-up toilet paper had been exchanged for gauze, my mouth was stuffed, and mascara smeared and stained to my face from many tears. Having no concept of how badly my face had been hit, I was bloodied and shaking from the shock, strapped down on a board, and now, laughing. I heard another laugh and realized Alyssa was actually in the same ambulance with me. With all the commotion, I assumed she had been taken to the hospital already and was so happy to find out we were still together. Trying to see her out of the corner of my eye while being strapped to a stretcher, and her trying to eye me too, we

found some relief and light-heartedness in the comical of the moment.

Just being together, and being able to laugh in the condition we were in, that was the first moment I remember talking to God. I thanked Him for protecting us from further harm and acknowledged His presence and peace with us.

Healing Takes Time

Not being able to work right after the accident, my life revolved around doctors' appointments. It was such a frustrating time. I had experienced the worst thing that had ever happened to me, and in the weeks that followed, I had to continuously relive it as I went to each appointment, or in every moment where I couldn't do something for myself because I wasn't physically able to.

My wrist didn't heal for six months, and half of that time I was in a cast. My teeth restoration work took roughly the same time, with different stages as my mouth had to heal. Though my stitches came out of my lip within a few weeks, it would take a year's time for the tissue to be healed completely. It took time for my feet to heal enough to where I could put normal pressure on them or to even wear shoes, let alone dance or run again. My body healed with time, but even to this day there's ramifications from that accident I live with.

Physical healing wasn't the only healing to be done either. My heart and mind had to heal as well. I didn't want to be a victim of what had happened, but some days were just plain hard. Now, having lived through something physically, emotionally, and mentally traumatic, I feel I have so much more empathy for those who suffer from traumatic experiences. People may see your pain in the moment of the trauma, but they don't see the behind the scenes of the healing process, the extent of it, and at times how excruciating, trying, and lonely it can be.

But from the moment of injury and into the months of healing ahead, I made the decision to be an overcomer. My accident wasn't life-threatening, but I didn't want to use it as a crutch either. I chose to believe that this would not be something that had knocked me down and would be my undoing, but instead, something that God would use for good, and in some way, raise me higher.

Take Me High

Two days before my accident, I had been watching that week's broadcast of *American Idol* where one of the contestants sang "Love Came Down" by Kari Jobe. At that time, I was in a place where I felt like I really needed God's guidance in my life, and in that moment, the song touched my heart and spoke to me. Feeling God's presence, it brought me to a place of seeking God in my circumstances. Along with an excerpt

from *Jesus Calling's* daily devotion, I wrote out the lyrics of the song in my journal that night. I didn't know it then, but that song would become the anthem to my season of healing.

April 10, 2013

"*Trust Me in every detail of your life. Nothing is random in My kingdom. Everything that happens fits into a pattern for good, to those who love Me... I lifted you up out of the mire into My marvelous light. Having sacrificed My very life for you, I can be trusted in every facet of your life.*" - Jesus Calling

So much can happen in one night. I'll find out soon enough where and what direction my life will be headed next. I'm not trying to worry or stress. One minute I think everything will stay the same and the next minute I'm thinking everything is about to change. Lord, you know.

God, give me the strength I need. Be my Strength and my Peace.

"If my heart is overwhelmed and I cannot hear Your voice, I'll hold on to what is true, though I cannot see. If the storms of life they come, and the road ahead gets steep, I will lift these hands in faith. I will believe. I remind myself of all that You've done and the life I have because of Your son. Love came down and rescued me. Love came down and set me free. I am Yours. I am forever Yours. Mountain high

or valley low, I sing out and remind my soul, I am Yours, I am forever Yours."

The next time I would look at my journal, a mere five days later, I would see those last words penned, having had no idea at the time of writing them down how unknowingly intentional they would be for the days to come. I took comfort in it, that at a moment of desiring deep connection with God and searching for Him, He soon would also use that time to bring me solace and hope. I describe it as comfort, solace and hope, but words can only say so much and in my heart, it means so much more. He already knew what was to come.

God could have stopped my accident from happening, no doubt. And I believe God is more than able to and does orchestrate different situations in our lives, but I also believe that living in a fallen world, there are circumstances that take place God does not necessarily orchestrate, but allows. In so allowing, He can work through the circumstance to bring good from it. I believe my accident was such.

April 15, 2013

I wrote that last prayer to You not knowing what this past weekend would hold. I could have never guessed it would involve me getting hit by a car while walking across the crosswalk. But You were there. I couldn't see You or touch You, but I knew You were with us. Thank You Jesus.

"Trust Me and don't be afraid. Many things feel out of control.... When you are shaken out of your comfortable routines, grip My hand tightly and look for growth opportunities. Instead of bemoaning the loss of your comfort, accept the challenge of something new. I lead you on from glory to glory, making you fit for My kingdom. Say yes to the ways I work in your life. Trust Me, and don't be afraid." - Jesus Calling

"Mountain high or valley low, I sing out and remind my soul, I am Yours, I am forever Yours."

In the days that followed, life became a battle and juxtaposition of strength versus weakness, and faith versus doubt. As an optimist and "bright-side" believer, my natural inclination is to believe the best and to stand in unshakable faith that God is good and working all things for my good, relying on His strength in my weakness. And yet, I am only human. Days would come where there would be doubt and insecurities about my present and future, even while holding on to the firm belief that God was in fact working in my life and redeeming the things I had lost.

In a week's time, I was surprised at how fast my beaten body could heal some of the visible injuries I had. After wounds turned to scabs, some having already healed completely, I remember doing my makeup for the first time since the accident, feeling more like myself again, and choosing to see beauty. The stitches in my lip by this time were seemingly

unnoticeable, and while my gums and fractures healed, I had temporary teeth put in that covered the open wounds in my mouth, so they weren't exposed anymore. Especially at a time like this, the little details counted for a whole lot.

April 19, 2013

"Mountain high or valley low, I sing out and remind my soul, I am Yours."

*Lord, that's exactly what I need to keep doing — remind myself who You are and all You've done. It's been a rough week, beginning the healing process, accepting what's happened and that it's going to take a while for things to get back to normal — but I am **alive**. I am still here. You still have work for me to do; You're not finished with me yet.*

*God, rebuild this body of mine. Make me stronger, more resilient, and fearless. I don't know why last Friday night happened, but I know **You are working** all things out for my good and Your glory. And in time I will look back on this moment and see Your fingerprints in every inch of my story. I just don't have the eyes to see yet, but one day I'll be reminded of Your love and faithfulness in my greatest hour of need.*

"Love came down and rescued me. Love came down and set me free. I am Yours."

This is my prayer and praise in advance: for all You've done, are doing, and for all I have yet to see.

With much time on my hands to replay the past two weeks, I began to see more and more how blessed I was to be dealing with only these injuries and nothing more serious. Having the time to really think through what all had happened, I also sensed spiritual warfare as if Satan himself really was trying to bring me down, and I began to understand that there was more to my story than just a literal fall. Perhaps more than ever, I chose to believe God's purpose for me led to a greater destiny than even I could know. Having not realized it before, upon reflecting on previous journal entries, I realized it had been a year to date from my accident, April 12th, that I had established and written With All Her Might's mission statement and core values. Now, I saw more clearly that my accident was spiritual warfare, and not wanting to give Satan the upper-hand, I tried my best to not bemoan my circumstances, but instead, conquer them.

April 23, 2013

I'm ready to take Satan down.

God-strong,

With All Her Might

God had given me "Love Came Down" as my anthem and as I continued day by day in the healing process and moving forward with my life, it seemed as if every time I picked up *Jesus Calling* it spoke right to my soul and were the exact words I needed to hear for the moment I was in.

April 29, 2013

"Let Me teach you thankfulness. Begin by acknowledging that everything — all your possessions and all that you are — belongs to Me... If you slow down your pace of life, you can find Me anywhere. Some of My most precious children have been laid aside in sick beds or shut away in prisons. Others have voluntarily learned the discipline of spending time alone with Me. The secret of being thankful is learning to see everything from My perspective..." - *Jesus Calling*

Lord, meet me where I'm at. Instead of Satan using this accident as a way to attack and bring me down, Lord, rebuild and restore.

*Let this only make me **stronger** and **fearless**.*

One thing that I love about God is that He never leaves me without something to hold onto, even in the dark. During this time, in my heart I had already resolved the outcome of my accident: victory. Victory in overcoming defeat, and triumph in not allowing setbacks to keep me

from my God-given destiny. Though there was still pain, my heart began to gain so much hope and momentum. I was convinced that God would give beauty for ashes.

May 10, 2013

"As for me, I look to the Lord for his help. I wait confidently for God to save me, and my God will certainly hear me. Do not gloat over me, my enemies! Though I fall, I will rise again. Though I sit in darkness, the Lord himself will be my light." - Micah 7:7-8

It's past three in the morning and I haven't been able to sleep. I keep going back to the accident and everything that I'm dealing with now because of it.

Lord, only You can calm my anxious heart and dry my tears. Only You can give me lasting peace. I'm here God, meet me where I'm at.

In many ways that first month was a continuous but methodical timeline, visiting doctor after doctor waiting for status updates and evidence of restoration. And now, as boring and frustrating as it was, I had to wait until my body progressively healed.

May 12, 2013

It's been a month since the accident and I'm so tired of feeling this way. Lord, I just want things to go back to the way they were. I know someday they will, but at the same time, things will never be the same. How could they?

"You are among these weary ones, who are like wounded soldiers needing R&R. Take time to rest in the Love-Light of My Presence. I will gradually restore to you the energy that you have lost... Come to Me, all you who are weary and burdened, and you will find rest for your souls." - Jesus Calling

Resilience is bouncing back from unfavorable and harsh circumstances. It's being brought to my breaking point and recovering from it, to the point of it growing my inner strength and endurance. To be resilient is to persevere. I will persevere.

Thank you, Lord, for this time with You. I have fallen, but You've shown me I will also rise again. You're making me resilient — one day at a time.

God used people and occurrences to speak to and encourage me during my journey of healing, and then there were people who would intentionally or not, speak doubt and negativity to me. I remember talking with an acquaintance who knew I was in the accident. Without soliciting it, they advised me that I should be angry and go after the lady

who hit me. It was frustrating and deceptive at the same time. I wasn't carrying anger, bitterness or resentment toward the driver. Of course, I didn't want to be in the set of circumstances I found myself in, and I would sometimes upset myself when I would over-think my circumstances, but those negative emotions were never even a thought toward her. It did, however, upset me in the moment that an outsider who didn't really know me, my thoughts, or even full the circumstance thought they could tell me what the best thing to do was, but God gives grace for that too. And in a world full of negativity, full of hurt and broken people who in turn want others to share the hurt and brokenness they feel, it was a sign to let God use my accident and to shine His light through me and my circumstances even more so. I would not give pain for pain. My story would be different.

Declaring God's plans, promises and provisions over my life were what kept me going. And it was my alone time with Him, me and Him without the rest of the world, that meant the most. At the end of the day, I knew it was God alone who could identify with, understand, and know me better than anyone.

May 14, 2013

*"I am Almighty God. **Nothing is too difficult for Me.** I have chosen to use weak ones like you to accomplish My purposes. Your weakness is designed to open you up*

to My Power. Therefore, do not fear your limitations or measure the day's demands against your strength. What I require of you is to stay connected to Me, living in trusting dependence on My limitless resources... I am not a careless God. When I allow difficulties to come into your life, I equip you fully to handle them. Relax in My Presence, trusting in My Strength." - *Jesus Calling*

Last night I was so stressed and worried. I started thinking about all the "what-ifs". It's exhausting, Lord. I can't live like this, and I refuse to go on this way.

I talked with Emily tonight for a while and that was really encouraging and helped me to refocus and redirect my hope and trust in You. God, I don't want to be like the rest of the world, I don't want to be greedy. This isn't going to be like every other case out there: **This one is Yours.**

From the beginning You've been with me. You were there as me and Alyssa crossed the street and when we got knocked down, and You'll be there to see us rise from this and be overcomers. This is a God-story, because You make good from what was intended to harm, and You will lead us to a **glorious victory.**

You've always been my Provider, and no matter how the settlement turns out, I will praise You. It's not about the money, Lord, it's about trusting You to provide all my needs. Continue to give me Your peace and continue to strengthen me and remind

me of Your gracious favor. You know there will be days ahead I will need the constant reminders.

But thank You, Lord. Thank You for saving me, protecting me from worse damage and injuries, for pouring love and support into my life, and for giving me this season to really trust You and know You, and to be able to truly live out what it means to be a **fearless** Woman of God.

I read Psalm 143 this morning and it fit perfectly to my life with what's been happening this past month.

This is what it means to be Fearless: to live life standing tall, head held high, though surrounded by fearful circumstances. To be an overcomer, to be resilient.

With All Her Might

My journal entries to come followed suit, filled with hope while countering doubt, relying on God yet also wondering how He would work things out fully and when. It may sound repetitive because it was. But isn't that life as well? The constant highs and lows, ups and downs, and the choices we make to trust and believe or to worry and doubt.

"Hear my prayer, O Lord; listen to my plea! Answer me because you are faithful and righteous. Don't bring your servant to trial! Compared to you, no one is perfect. My enemy has chased me. He has knocked me to the ground. He forces me to live in darkness like those in the grave. I am losing all hope; I am paralyzed with fear. I remember the days of old. I ponder all your great works. I think about what you have done. I reach out for you. I thirst for you as parched land thirsts for rain. Come quickly, Lord, and answer me, for my depression deepens. Don't turn away from me or I will die. Let me hear of your unfailing love to me in the morning, for I am trusting you. Show me where to walk, for I have come to you in prayer. Save me from my enemies, Lord; I run to you to hide me. Teach me to do your will, for you are my God. May your gracious spirit lead me forward on a firm footing. For the glory of your name, O Lord, save me. In your righteousness, bring me out of this distress. In your unfailing love, cut off all my enemies and destroy all my foes, for I am your servant." - Psalm 143

Accepting the Broken, Seeing the Beautiful

I will say it again that I am undoubtedly grateful my injuries were not more extensive, but in my humanness, it has also been a fight to always fully accept them. The worst thing that happened to me that night wasn't breaking my wrist, or even busting my lip. The worst thing that happened to me was getting my two teeth knocked out.

When I finally came to after being hit, I was lying on the asphalt. Using my left hand to prop myself up, I noticed the blood coming from my mouth and clasped it. Feeling with my tongue to find the source, I felt the noticeable gaps between a couple of teeth. All I could cry out was, "My teeth!" I cried not only from the realization of being hit and reacting to the sight of my wounds, but also and especially to the fact that my teeth I had prized and cherished were now gone forever.

Having always loved to laugh and smile, and having always prided myself in my smile, I was in immediate disbelief and devastated. When I was younger, I didn't need braces except for minor cosmetic reasons. My parents couldn't afford them at the time, but that didn't keep me from wanting them. I had a dream of having a perfect smile. It was always something very important to me, I loved to smile and wanted to be proud of it.

I'll never forget that summer morning before starting my junior year of high school. My mom came into my bedroom

and woke me up with the news that I was going to get braces. That moment meant so much to me. My parents didn't have to spend their hard-earned money on braces, but they chose to and did it for me. I had always taken good care of my teeth, but I took even better care once I got my braces. My parents' sacrifice meant the world to me and I was going to honor that. So as bewildering as it sounds, in those seconds of realizing I had lost my teeth in the accident, it brought me back to that place of my parents' sacrifice and how five years after getting my braces off, this is what happens. It was unbelievably devastating.

Thankfully, the Monday after my accident, my family dentist whom I had known most of my life took me in right away to assess the damage. I remember him holding my face and grieving for me as he witnessed himself the extent of my injuries. Though not much could be done until my mouth healed more, I walked away from that appointment with temporary teeth that looked good and were fashioned to fit my injuries. In the months during the restoration period to follow, almost every dentist appointment I was given new temporaries until my gums and mouth were fully healed to do the permanent work.

Though I was grateful to have the restoration work done, it was still hard to accept that some of my teeth were gone forever and from now on, my smile would never be what it once was. Because of these insecurities, I was embarrassed at times to talk or smile. Friends and family would tell

me they couldn't notice but I would think, how could they not? A conversation I had with a coworker was sweet and encouraging. I had finally shared with her that I was embarrassed and insecure about the appearance of my teeth and sometimes it made me second-guess smiling or not, though I always tried to opt for a smile. She, like everyone else, said she couldn't really notice. Then she also shared that it was my choice to not let what had happened steal my joy, and to remind myself that no one and nothing could take that away from me. I knew that in my heart, but sometimes it was a battle to be brave and show it with my smile.

In late October, just over six months after my accident, I finally received my permanents and was done with the restoration process. It was so nice to be finished, yet at the same time, I continued to have trouble seeing my new teeth as beautiful as my original, and still over the years, had insecurities about them.

If I were to ever doubt God's concern over the little details in our lives, my teeth would be a prime example of His care. I can't recall how many times over the years since my accident people have commented on my teeth and how beautiful they are. Even with compliments, I would still question if people were seeing what I saw. If you looked, you could see apparent flaws with my teeth, yet that didn't stop friends, family, acquaintances or even strangers from complementing them. Those were precious reminders to me from God that my smile was "still just as beautiful", as one

friend put it. And maybe the greatest lesson learned of all was that it wasn't the display of teeth that created the beauty, but the genuine heart behind a smile.

Three years later, after receiving my permanent teeth, I eventually had to restart the restoration process over because of an infection. To this day, I am still in the process of having the follow-up work done. Sometimes it is frustrating to think about and it makes me wish none of this had ever happened because then at least I would have my natural teeth that I was happy with and were problem-free, yet I try to count my blessings and be accepting of where I am at in the process. Now, while waiting for my permanents a second time, I do feel grateful that my teeth and smile have once again become something that I love and am proud of.

When I fractured my wrist, I broke my scaphoid (navicular) bone, one of the eight small bones in the wrist that is extremely difficult to heal, yet commonly fractured by falling on an outstretched hand. My first appointment with the doctor, he told me that if the bone didn't heal I would need surgery, and even if it did heal, I might still need surgery down the road. It was a scary thought at first, but it was something that my family and I, and others around me took to prayer. I didn't want surgery. I knew God could heal me and believed He would. The first two weeks I was in a full-arm cast that drove me crazy and led to many sleepless nights. Thankfully, after that my wrist showed signs of healing and my full-arm cast was replaced with a smaller,

more freeing one. I remember just being so grateful that I had the use and mobility of my elbow back once more.

After three months, though there were significant signs of improvement, my wrist still hadn't healed completely. The doctor said it wasn't healthy for my arm to be in a cast for any longer, so he took it off and I would continue the healing process in a brace instead. What a shock it was to see how my hand and arm had atrophied and changed in those three months, but I was so glad to have it gone and was anxious to see my arm return to its normal appearance. Another three months later, I went to my last appointment at the doctor's office where I was pronounced healed with the doctor still warning of the possibility of surgery and arthritis. My wrist still hurts at times and I can't use it to the extent I once did, but honestly, I am just thankful God healed me and I didn't need surgery. And I am believing Him for no surgery in my future as well.

Most marks and scars on my body from the accident have faded away completely or are barely visible anymore, but one permanently remains and the basis behind *Beauty Marks* lies in it. That night, I didn't have a clue of how impactful that one little injury would have on me as I moved forward with my life, especially compared to my wrist or teeth. Before I got to the hospital, I hadn't realized that my lip was busted. I assumed all the blood from my mouth was coming from having lost my teeth. I still remember the doctor in the emergency room on duty that night and

tending to my injuries numbing my lip before taking the needle to stitch me up. As he sewed, my view of the lighted ceiling was covered up by his head hovering over mine to do the work. I remember when I first saw him he reminded me of a famous actor, and then as he began to sew, seeing the sweat beading his forehead, I wondered the difficulty and skill it took for a doctor to stitch up skin.

After it was done, I honestly thought nothing of the stitches and assumed my lip would heal back to its normal state, being none the wiser until two days later when I went back to the hospital for a check-up. It wasn't the same doctor who had seen me in the emergency room, but this new doctor when examining my stitches told me the previous one had done a good job sewing my lip and it should heal normally. As he said those words, the first fear about my lip formed, is it possible it would never look the same?

My lip healed, but no, it has never been the same. My scar isn't dramatic, most people when looking at me probably wouldn't even know or be able to tell, but it's still a scar. At times I would refer to it as my "hook lip", as if it had been baited and snagged with proof of the damage. I can't say how many tears I've cried over the years because of that tiny, little scar. Many times I've looked at my reflection in the mirror and having really taken notice of it, brings me back to that night. It's a result of that night, as if my story is now woven into my scar. Sometimes it's hard to not get emotional, and

at other times, I can give it a simple touch with my finger and move on with my day.

It's not that I can't get the work done either. Several months after my accident I had a consultation with a plastic surgeon. He said I would need a full year for the tissue to heal before I could do anything to it, but it wouldn't be a problem for him to fix it back to normal. At first, I debated having the work done and then I made peace with it. I made the decision that this is *my* Beauty Mark and chose to see it as a visible reflection of my saving grace.

I remember being at a church retreat several years before my accident. One of the girls there wasn't yet a believer, but she was seeking God out. She had recently been in a car accident, one that probably should have taken her life or at the very least done more damage, but instead she walked away from it, the only mark being on her chest from where her seat belt held her back. I remember her crying and saying that she didn't know why more hadn't happened to her, but she had this mark. That mark saved her.

Maybe one day I'll get the work done and have a perfected lip, but I don't really know and don't really think about it. When I see my mark, I think about the accident, but more importantly I try to focus on the grace and the redemption in it. By God's grace I'm still here, I am healthy, and I am whole. I don't necessarily like my scar, but I also can't help but see the beauty in it. If there is something to love about it, it reminds me of With All Her Might's logo, a blossoming

and breaking-free butterfly, and at other times, I see a heart. My scar is proof there was ever a wound to begin with, but I can see the beautiful in it because it is also evidence of healing. That may be one of the most profound things I have relearned with my accident: if I have the eyes to see it, anything can become beautiful. And I see it as living proof that God truly does make all things beautiful in His time.

Fear is a Liar

When I declared 2013 my "Year of Fearlessness", I couldn't have known what all would occur in my life and how these circumstances would challenge my courage. If anything, I had naively assumed any adversity that might come my way would be from me trying to build up With All Her Might. I started the year writing a blog discussing my thoughts.

January 12, 2013

To be fearless means to be bold and to be resolute without fear. This doesn't mean that fear won't come, but that when it does, you don't avoid it or go around it; instead, you push courageously through it, knowing there is victory to be had if only you take that first step...

Sometimes we face things that seem too impossible, too big, or too scary to even know where to begin. Yet I believe in the core of who we are, we know; we know that if only we had the courage to take that first step to

begin, God would meet us, walk with us, and lead us to incredible victory... and we will see indescribable beauty.

After my accident, walking outside and on busy streets brought fear. I had never had to walk the streets of LA as much as I did during that time and had never been more paranoid in my life over it. Because of my cast, I was not allowed to drive so that when I went back to work, I inevitably had to take the Metro, Los Angeles' public transportation. In order for me to get to work each day in downtown LA, I had to walk outside my apartment, yards away from where my accident had taken place, then walk to the corner of Ventura and Sepulveda boulevards to catch a bus to the Universal City station. The irony of it was awful, but probably the best thing for me. Every day I went to work and came home I had to face my newly-developed fear of crossing the street. I was more cautious than ever looking both ways multiple times, checking over my shoulder while walking across to make sure no one was coming, all the while trying to look normal and easy going. But despite hating it in the beginning, it became a blessing in disguise and something that helped me overcome a fear shaped by my accident.

It was also a process to finally use the crosswalk that I had been hit in. I would've been alright with never using that crosswalk again, while at the same time, I didn't want it to hold any power or fear over me. I remember being emotional the first time crossing it, and the first couple times doing so,

but then I got as used to it as I could, not forgetting what had taken place there, but also not letting it affect my decision to move forward and use it.

Being fearless, when it came to my accident, meant trusting God with every part of it from start to finish, knowing He truly was taking care of it all. It also meant denying fear the power to hold any aspect of my accident over me, and that included so many things: my accident didn't define me or my future, I was not a victim to it but instead an overcomer, I would be healed and healed completely, God would use this for something good and raise me higher. This was not an ending but a twist to my story.

I knew fear wasn't from God and I didn't want to give the room to Satan or self-doubt to roam in it. In many ways I think fear is inevitable, there will always be circumstances or the potential of circumstances that are frightening, but it was my choice to allow fear to have the power, or to claim that power for myself. Some days I admittedly faced defeat, especially when worrying about my healing progression, and other days I was overwhelmed with the joy of victory for not allowing fear to get the best of me, but instead conquering it. It was a battle, but it fashioned resilience.

Fear Less

Five years after my accident, 2018 became a first in that I repeated in naming a year. It was my "Year of the Fearless"

once more, and my quest to finally write *Beauty Marks* was inspiration to my resolve. My heart had become so weary of fighting, procrastinating, and downright ignoring the call to write this. I was determined to finish it, and in so doing, fulfill a vision and desire God had placed in me.

A fear that had kept me from writing *Beauty Marks* for so long is the thought of, why me? Why should my story be told more than others? In short, it shouldn't. This was originally intended to be (and still will be) a collection of stories from women who bear their own Beauty Marks. Yet over the years having held off the call to write, when I got serious about writing it and settled in to start the process, my convictions told me that *Beauty Marks* should first come from me, and from a place of vulnerability. Let me open my heart first, and from one soul to another, share mine.

Up until this point in my life, I have kept my accident quite protected from the outside world. Inevitably news originally spread through family and friends to acquaintances, coworkers, prayer circles and the like, but as far as me telling my own story, only those close to me or with whom I have felt safe with has it ever been privately shared. It was something so personal, so intimately devastating, I didn't want to share it with the whole world. I felt like if I did, I would be giving away part of my story that others who barely knew me didn't deserve to know.

Another significant reason why I never opened up about it was because again, I felt as if in doing so it would give power to the accident, and I didn't want that. There is no doubt that my accident altered my life in various ways, but I especially didn't want to put it in writing, as if it was permanent. Even though I included journal entries in this, not once did I ever journal about everything that happened that night. To me, words are life, and I didn't want to write out the details that had been so traumatic and tragic to me.

Yet I always knew there would come a time. I knew a time would come when I would be ready to share my story on my own accord. Not to give power to it, but to tell of the other side of the tragic: the outcomes are what we make them to be. God brings redemption and we are the bearers.

Traces of Grace

"If you forgive anyone's sins, they are forgiven. If you refuse to forgive them, they are unforgiven." – John 20:23

Monday morning following my accident, I received a call from the lady who had hit Alyssa and I. Having acquired our contact information from one of the policemen at the scene, she called both of us to see how we were doing. She apologized again and shared with me her perspective of the incident and described how she just didn't see us walking. She told me that if I was mad and wanted to yell and scream at her or if I hated her, I could and that she understood.

I don't remember how emotional I was on the phone, or she, but I do remember telling her my thoughts of what had

happened. I shared with her that even though I hated what had happened to me, I did not hate her. I said that even though I was injured, I was believing God to heal me and had faith He would use the accident for something good. She then said if I needed anything to not hesitate to call her.

Much like sharing my story, there would come a time, I knew, that I would want to talk to her again. After everything was said and done, after all my injuries were healed and case closed, I felt a time would come where there would be only one thing left to do. I would see her and get closure in a sense, then leave in peace with my accident's story at its end.

It happened to be one year later almost to the day we met. When I called her she knew exactly who I was and without hesitation agreed to meet. We were together for maybe an hour. We talked about ourselves a bit, and then we talked about that night. More than anything, I wanted her to know that night didn't put a permanent scar on my life and in many ways, I had already seen God do incredible things in and through it. I wanted her to know that there was never bitterness or hate, but grace and forgiveness. When we said goodbye, I left knowing I would never see her again.

"The next time you see or think of the one who broke your heart, look twice. As you look at his face, look also for His face – the face of the One who forgave you. Look into the eyes of the king who wept when you pleaded for mercy. Look into the face of the Father who gave you grace when no one else gave you a chance… And then, because God has forgiven you more than you'll ever be called on to forgive in another, set your enemy – and yourself – free."

- *Everyday Blessings*, Max Lucado

II

For the Wounded

"You were young, you were free, and you dared to believe
You could be the girl who could change the world.
Then your life took a turn, and you fell, and it hurt.
But you're still that girl and you're
gonna change this world."

– *Still That Girl*, Britt Nicole

My first purpose in writing this book was to share from my story. As our lives unfold, so too do our chapters marked by passing seasons. We all have the opportunity to tell our stories, and as a follower of Christ, I see that as a responsibility and privilege to tell the world what God has done in my life, one marked with grace, beauty, and redemption.

You have your own story to share with the world too, chapters already written and those yet to be lived. Maybe you've never gone through a similar circumstance like mine, or maybe yours is much, much worse. As mentioned before, something that kept me from writing for so long was the dreaded question of, why tell such a minimal story as my own when there were more impactful ones to share? But whether you think your story is big or small, it is meaningful nonetheless, and only yours to tell.

While walking out the reality of my accident, during the healing process, and now to looking back over the last six years and seeing how far I've come, I want to share what I have learned through it all.

You Do Not Owe the World Your Story

Having just said that we all have the opportunity to tell our stories, it doesn't mean that you have to. There is wisdom in knowing when, with whom, and to what extent you share about your life.

I can recall a time or two where I opened up about

my accident to others, not feeling completely comfortable with those I was surrounded by. Once I was with a group of acquaintances on our way to lunch. We were walking on a busy street and they wanted to jaywalk to get to the restaurant. Not wanting to be a pain but at the same time not feeling comfortable jaywalking, I briefly mentioned being in an accident and wanting to be safe as we crossed (though the irony of the story is I actually was hit in a crosswalk). We ended up going to a crosswalk, but I had peaked the interest for a few questions to come up. Though I answered, I tried to give short responses without sounding too bothered. It was my story to tell, but I didn't want people who only barely knew me to know something so personal that had happened to me without understanding the significance of me sharing it with them.

As I wrote this book, without naming every detail of my accident or the months of healing to follow, I wanted to be true to what had happened. I have spoken about this through With All Her Might, that I believe we can be vulnerable and still maintain our innocence. By this I mean, when we're sharing precious details of our stories, we don't have to feel stripped of our dignity to do so. You do not owe the world an explanation. What you share is your choice alone to make.

Maybe I could have described my accident with a much more detailed account, but it wouldn't have changed the narrative for the better, and in doing so would have only left me feeling impudently overexposed. There is wisdom in how

we use our words and to what extent. Words are powerful, words are life.

Similarly, be wise with whom you let into your circle and speak into your life. Although at times I couldn't help but run into people who would speak negativity and feelings of bitterness, those closest to me were my support system that spoke life and truth to my accident and my healing process.

Your Circumstances ≠ Your Identity

As a child of God, your identity isn't something to be discovered, it is your birthright. Standing firm in your identity is of utmost importance because the foundation for your life and worldview is found in it. For as you view yourself, you will also see the world and events that happen to you or that transpire around you.

I have talked openly about not allowing my accident to define me or my future. I believe there were many opportunities to allow my circumstances to affect the well-being of my spiritual, physical, emotional, and mental health in a negative way. I talk about it being a battle with myself to not give in to feeling like a victim or enslaved to my situation. We can show ourselves acceptance and self-love without wallowing in and hiding behind our circumstances. If we come to terms that we are not our circumstances, we ready ourselves for victory from them, as if proclaiming that the things that happen to us and in our lives have an expiration

date. They do not define us and aren't our permanent and true identity.

The mind is such a powerful thing. What we believe and hold onto can have a huge impact on our lives, for better or worse, and our minds play a key role in reminding us of our identity. When we identify as children of God, it is important to remind ourselves of what that means, and what that title holds. When we reflect on what the Bible says about who we are as God's children, we prepare our mind and soul, head and heart for anything that comes our way.

See Your Beauty

"God only creates beauty." I don't know where I heard this or if I just started saying it myself, but for years this is always my answer when the question of appearance comes up. We are all "fearfully and wonderfully made" (Psalm 139:14). Every person is undeniably beautiful because they were created by God and made in His image. I love these verses in Genesis that prove it:

"So God created people in his own image; God patterned them after himself; male and female he created them... Then God looked over all he had made, and he saw that it was excellent in every way." - Genesis 1:26, 31

Inner beauty will always be unarguably more important than outer beauty, but I'd be lying if I said my outer looks and body image didn't matter to me. I know it doesn't amount to

everything, but I still want to see myself as beautiful when I look in the mirror. After my accident and before my face had healed, it was hard to see myself and accept just how ugly the damage was. But even if some features were never to go back to the way they were before, I knew that regardless, my face didn't define me, and as I mentioned, I wanted to see my Beauty Marks for what they were: proof of God's grace and healing in my life.

You may have marks that you bear too, and yours may have cut much deeper than mine, standing out and on display for all to see. Whether acquired in your lifetime or something you were born with, regardless of the imperfections you see when you look in the mirror, you are undeniably and indisputably beautiful. And if I could give something to you now, it would be the confidence and assurance to truly know and accept the beauty of who you are and who God has created you to be, inside and out.

Be Fearless in Faith

"What is faith? It is the confident assurance that what we hope for is going to happen. It is the evidence of things we cannot yet see." - Hebrews 11:1

Many well-known and widely-circulated inspirational quotes speak truth when defining courage as doing something in spite of fear. Being fearless doesn't necessarily mean then that there is a lack of fear, but instead, the choice to move

forward despite its threatening conditions. Fear is meant to keep us frozen, unable or unwilling to move forward, and keeps us from our destiny. When we cry out to God and search the Bible for encouragement, strength, and courage to get through the darkness, we can hold onto and find comfort in His promises. Some of my favorite scriptures I read to remind myself of these promises and to declare over my life are:

- "For I know the plans I have for you, declares the Lord. Plans to prosper you and not to harm you, plans to give you hope and a future." - Jeremiah 29:11 NIV
- "And we know that God causes all things to work together for the good of those who love God and are called according to his purpose for them." - Romans 8:28
- "What can we say about such wonderful things as these? If God is for us, who can ever be against us?" - Romans 8:31
- "Can anything ever separate us from Christ's love? Does it mean he no longer loves us if we have trouble or calamity, or are persecuted, or are hungry or cold or in danger or threatened with death?... No, despite all these things, overwhelming victory is ours through Christ, who loved us. And I am convinced that nothing can ever separate us from his love. Death can't, and life can't. The angels can't, and the

demons can't. Our fears for today, our worries about tomorrow, and even the powers of hell can't keep God's love away. Whether we are high above the sky or in the deepest ocean, nothing in all creation will ever be able to separate us from the love of God that is revealed in Christ Jesus our Lord." - Romans 8:35, 37-39

- "Now glory be to God! By his mighty power at work within us, he is able to accomplish infinitely more than we could ever dare to ask or hope." - Ephesians 3:20

It has always been important to me to document my life and journey of faith through my journal. The biggest reason is to remember and to reflect in the days, months, and years to come how things have changed and to see how God worked in those circumstances that I had once thought so impossible.

When things happen, good or bad, reflect and take note of God's fingerprints in your life for you will undoubtedly see them. If we open our eyes to see how God is working now and has worked previously in our circumstances, it provides strength, courage, and endurance to walk through new ones, and produces resilience as we see His visible provisions. A huge factor in being able to trust God with my accident was because I had seen Him provide and take care of me so many times before. By remembering His faithfulness in the past,

we can trust Him to be there, guide us, and see us through our circumstances once more.

As a result of living in a fallen and sinful world, bad things happen, but it doesn't mean that God causes these things. They are the condition and state of the world we live in. God can choose to and sometimes does keep them from happening, but He can also choose to and sometimes does allow them. We can't forget that Satan can play a part in such occurrences as well. It is important for us to use discernment in recognizing what all is going on in our circumstances, what they are directed at, and where they are coming from.

With that said, as much as we want to choose and activate "fearless faith", it is a battle. Having faith and trying our best to keep courage doesn't guarantee a smooth and easy life. Life is messy, painful, and fear-invoking at times, but faith in God to be faithful to us is still a choice. It becomes our choice, then, to have faith and let the trials we walk through become something God changes and uses for good.

"We can rejoice, too, when we run into problems and trials, for we know that they are good for us – they help us learn to endure. And endurance develops strength of character in us, and character strengthens our confident expectation of salvation. And this expectation will not disappoint us. For we know how dearly God loves us, because he has given us the Holy Spirit to fill our hearts with his love." – Romans 5:3-5

Always Choose Grace

Bitterness, resentment, hatred, and unforgiveness are all poison and toxic to the mind, heart, body, and soul. The worst thing about it is the ones who hold onto these poisons are most hurting themselves, because it is rare that the person those feelings are directed toward would ever feel as much or hold onto them like the one engaging in them. But choosing grace lightens a heart, and forgiveness is freeing.

I understand there are contributing factors to my accident that probably made it easier to accept what had happened and forgive the driver, such as she actually stopped and didn't run from the accident, or the fact that she genuinely cared for mine and Alyssa's well-being. Regardless, my choice to forgive her wasn't made in the moments after my accident, but was a choice I made long ago when I chose to follow Jesus for the rest of my life.

"I tell you, her sins – and they are many – have been forgiven, so she has shown me much love. But a person who is forgiven little shows only little love." – Luke 7:47

When I realize the extent of my own sins and how God has forgiven each one, and still forgives me as I continue to live an imperfect life, forgiveness and grace become much easier to give away and are what I want to give and extend to others as well. When you have been shown much love and much grace, it is hard to keep it for yourself.

To my very core I am flawed, but I have never known

condemnation from God. People may choose to condemn, but God is ready and eager to accept you as-is with open arms and no preconditions. The things you may have gone through or are currently involved in may not seem so easy. Maybe unspeakably evil things have been said or done to you and you don't see how you could ever forgive and let go of what has happened and how you have been wronged. I don't claim to know what or how you are feeling. All I know is that forgiveness is possible, and only you can choose it for yourself, your situation, and to give it to those involved.

"And then, because God has forgiven you more than you'll ever be called on to forgive in another, set your enemy – and yourself – free."

Live Your Life

I've always been an advocate of living a full, meaningful life and making the most of the time given to us. I want to live out my purpose, the reason I was created, and make a difference. I want to know I lived not just for myself but for others as well, my accident only highlighted this more.

If we think of the time limit to our lives, eighty to ninety years if we make it that far, in light of eternity, there is no comparison. Our lives are so short, yet so precious, none of us are guaranteed more time than the moment we're in now. It can be a scary thing, but it can also motivate us to actually and truly *live*. If we have all of eternity waiting for us, how

can we not muster the courage to follow our dreams and live out our God-given calling today? This life is all we have to impact eternity.

My accident was never a death-defying experience, but I know God did protect me from further harm. After hearing countless stories since of pedestrians losing their lives to being hit by a car, I thank God every time, that I am still here. And if you ever have experienced something traumatic, something that you walked away from, you have to believe that God is saying there is more to your story than what has been written. There is more to come for you.

If you are alive, if you are breathing, you have purpose. If you are alive, if you are breathing, there are plans God made that *you* are meant to fulfill. If you are alive, if you are breathing, God's calling in your life is still unfinished. Don't leave your story unwritten.

Wait for Redemption

"I am holding you by your right hand – I, the Lord your God. And I say to you, 'Do not be afraid. I am here to help you... I am the Lord, your Redeemer.'" - Isaiah 41:13-14

This passage has always held significance to me and I've often thought about the Bible speaking of God's "victorious right hand" and how He holds us by the right hand. There was always so much beauty, mystery, and comfort in those words. They were so specific, but never did they mean more

to me than after my accident. When I reflect on that moment of being hit and the impact of it, in my mind I have a clear vision of how it played out, though I will never fully know. I blacked out and will never fully know the exact details, but my perspective goes beyond the visible eye.

The way I see it being played out is the image of God by my side, holding my right hand, while stopping the force of the impact from hurting me further, shielding me with His victorious right hand. Perhaps this is a coping mechanism, but I still see its significance. The message I see in it is God allowing something bad to happen, but also intervening as if to say, this will hurt you and affect you, but I am with you and I will not let it kill you. That image for me has always been such a powerful and comforting thing.

"You intended to harm me but God meant it for good, to accomplish what is now being done, the saving of many lives." - Genesis 50:20 NIV

When you believe that God is taking care of you, you are also believing and choosing to identify how any occurrence in your life can be used by God for a greater purpose. And the beautiful thing about redemption is that it often includes more than just you as a recipient of the blessings and benefits. God has a way of using the awful and tragic in our lives to not only redeem us, but to free others as well.

"God has made everything beautiful for its own time." - Ecclesiastes 3:11

From the beginning I chose to believe that God was

working in the midst of the chaos from my accident and waited to see redemption for my wounds. Holding onto God's promises and waiting on redemption is choosing to see the beautiful before it's been established. It is seeing the mess of many pieces and parts being thrown together and waiting to see them fit to create a masterpiece. Look for God in your circumstances and believe He is working, even if you can't see it yet. It is God's nature to give beauty for ashes.

Live Healed

Every personal story of hurt, tragedy, and trauma all holds value and significance. But from my experience, God has taught me that the power doesn't lie in the tragic, the power lies in how we choose to respond to and live out the outcomes. If our identity is not founded in the things that happen to us, then a progression of moving away and moving forward from those things that have harmed us is possible, and it is ultimately our choice to live healed.

There are different types of healing: spiritual, mental, physical, emotional, etc. With my accident, God healed my physical body, but He also had to heal the emotional and mental wounds I was left with from the trauma. Healing isn't one-size-fits-all and we all heal in our own timeframes, but it is our choice in accepting and embracing healing and living it out, or not.

Especially after the physical healing I went through, my

accident was never part of my every day conversation. It was something that happened to me, but it was not something I was going to carry the weight of daily for the rest of my life. I would be in denial to say it didn't affect my life, I have the scars for proof. But to carry the emotional burden and mental trauma with me for the rest of my life, or to give it to God instead, that was my choice, and I chose to let God heal my inner wounds as well.

Healing can take time, but it's not healing if we're willfully carrying around our wounds where there should be Beauty Marks. We don't have to be afraid of scars. Our scars are evidence of our healing. Let God restore you, body, mind, heart, and soul, and live healed.

III

All Things Redeemed

"Now you will see what I will do…"

- Exodus 6:1

With All Her Might was created in 2011 and first established in 2012 as an organization whose sole purpose was to create a community for women with a mission to "encourage, strengthen, and inspire every woman who desires to actively, fearlessly, and passionately pursue her God-given calling in life, love, and dreams." What that looked like to a college student with little to no disposable income meant having a couple gatherings at my apartment where friends could come together and just share, being open about life and the struggles we face, and finding encouragement through community. It also meant lending my voice to write the things God was teaching me in my life through my blog, *Confessions of a Broken Heart.* I had a dream to be used by God to speak life and truth to others and to write what all God had placed in my heart, and this was my starting point.

Fast forward a year. Now, as a recent college graduate, I celebrated each accomplishment and move toward the direction of my dreams. I appreciated the journey of my progress, especially since it had stemmed from little beginnings. So when my accident happened a few months after my move to LA, it was a natural response to question the direction my life would take next. But believing God to make beautiful and bring redemption from my scars, I had the vision of my accident being what would catapult With All Her Might and become a driving force of perseverance and resilience to hold on to my dreams and see with my own eyes, them come to life.

In early July, almost three months since my accident, I was unexpectedly given the greatest opportunity to travel to Europe to speak, perform, and teach dance workshops at a German youth leadership conference in the Netherlands. My friend, Sandra, who had supported my vision for With All Her Might from the start, had initiated the opportunity for me to go. I had never been given an opportunity of the like and it was no less than a dream come true. The preceding months had been so trying. I hadn't let go of trusting God, but I also didn't know why He was giving me such an incredible opportunity. And yet, I think He couldn't have shown me in any greater way that He was taking care of me, and it was just the beginning of His redemption for my wounds.

God brought me to many places after my initial trip to Europe where I had the privilege of sharing my heart and story through speaking engagements for With All Her Might, and sometimes that included me being vulnerable with strangers and sharing about my accident. In the fall of 2013, it was With All Her Might's trip to Germany and the Netherlands. In 2014, With All Her Might was involved and represented at multiple festivals, a trip to Mexico, and a young women's conference. In 2015, it was going to Uganda and in 2016, it was another youth camp in Italy. And in 2017, it was representing With All Her Might in my first marathon and my return back to Uganda.

Let me put it on record for all to know, these things

happened because of God's grace and redemption in my life and only because of that. His faithfulness caused me to believe the darkness wouldn't last. I had seen God work in the past, but it wasn't until after my accident that I received all these huge blessings and amazing opportunities to travel for With All Her Might. I felt so undeserving, yet at the same time, I understood my accident was a wake-up call to recommit myself to fulfilling the purposes God has for me.

I could write story after story of how God brought redemption into my life after the accident and how He brought me to places and gave me opportunities I could only dream of, but the most important story to tell is the other purpose for this book: where He has my heart, and that is Uganda.

Redemption is Here

When I was eighteen years old I encountered a video that has forever changed my heart for the people of central and east Africa. I was so bothered by what I saw: war, corruption, disease, and poverty. I asked God to instill that ache in me for a lifetime if I was meant to do something about it, and over a decade later, it has never gone away. From that moment on, I always knew there would be a day that I would physically be there, in Africa. I can't count how many times over a period of eight years that God would speak to my heart about going, I would cry the experience was so real.

And I could be anywhere: one time I was in church, one time I was at a concert, one time I was waiting in my car for my brother to get off work. The places were random, but the message was the same. It was a knowing: I knew, that I knew, that I knew, God would lead me there one day.

In early 2013, while cleaning my office one day at work, I found a book called *Fulfilling Your God-Given Dreams*, by Bishop Patrick Okabe. When I asked my boss about it, she said it was written by a visiting Ugandan pastor who had actually preached a service at my work in the past. I was intrigued and interested in reading it, but it wasn't until after my accident and having the extra time to do so that I began it. As I read through the book, it touched my heart and was used by God to speak in my life and the circumstances I was facing at the moment: healing from my accident, believing God to restore what all had been broken, and raising me and His dreams for me to fulfillment. After I finished it, I had the desire to contact Bishop Okabe and inquire about visiting his ministry, Impact Ministries Uganda, which is a church with a school, orphanage, and radio station. But unsure if that was what I should do, and not wanting it to be my own desire, but God's, I waited over two years to write that email.

Thinking about writing to him every now and then, when 2015 came, my Year of Redemption, I couldn't shake the feeling that this would be my year to go as that desire kept growing in me and stirring my heart.

February 22, 2015

Today's message at church was exactly what I needed to hear, though I went in to the service not having a clue at how profound and impactful it would be. It was on "Thursday", and how the day is named after Thor, a protector. Pastor Hank proceeded to talk about God and the role God plays as Protector. He made it clear that God protects our soul, but in this life we are not always guaranteed protection from harm. He said Thursdays were a day for faith, that God protects our souls, and days of wisdom, that God gives us wisdom to keep us from harmful decisions and situations.

Pastor Hank said two things I really liked. First, he asked us if we ever thought about God asking the question, "Why are God's people afraid of bad things happening to them?" And the second thing was, "What would you do if you didn't let failure stop you?" His whole message centered around the idea that bad things are bound to happen in life, we're bound to get hurt, but it's not a bad thing to go through them if we allow God to use our circumstances to strengthen and grow us.

He also read Psalm 91. The second time he read it was at the end of the service, he asked us to close our eyes and meditate on the scripture and picture us in a place where God is speaking these words to us.

As those words were being spoken, I really felt like they were being spoken over my life in regards to Africa. I felt like God was consecrating me, that I was being consecrated to go to Africa. There have been so many times over the years I felt God speak to me about going, I believe it's getting closer and will be here soon!

I believed today God was telling me that He will be with me when I go and protect me, even if it's not in the way I think. It's sobering because I have to face the reality of safety concerns, but it's exciting because I know God will keep me where He has me. He will protect me. This means I'm still going, and soon!

There are two conversations that stand out during this time that really spoke to me and led me to write to the bishop. The first was an acquaintance with whom I went on a hike with that became one of those God-meetings where you share more with that person in a moment than you've shared over a lifetime with some. It was a divine moment where God used her to speak to me in a meaningful way about taking the next step and writing an email.

The second was an acquaintance from the Democratic Republic of the Congo whom I was eager to learn from about his life and ministry. I told him I had the desire to travel to Africa and I believed God placed it in my heart, but a huge reason that I had never gone was that so many people have gone before me, could I make a difference? And wouldn't the money

"Those who live in the shelter of the Most High will find rest in the shadow of the Almighty. This I declare of the Lord:

He alone is my refuge, my place of safety; he is my God and I'm trusting him. For he will rescue you from every trap and protect you from the fatal plague. He will shield you with his wings. He will shelter you with his feathers. His faithful promises are your armor and protection. Do not be afraid of the terrors of the night, nor fear the dangers of the day, nor dread the plague that stalks in darkness, nor the disaster that strikes at midday. Though a thousand fall at your side, though ten thousand are dying around you, these evils will not touch you. But you will see it with your eyes; you will see how the wicked are punished.

If you make the Lord your refuge, if you make the Most High your shelter, no evil will conquer you; no plague will come near your dwelling. For he orders his angels to protect you wherever you go. They will hold you with their hands to keep you from striking your foot on a stone. You will trample down lions and poisonous snakes; you will crush fierce lions and serpents under your feet.

The Lord says: I will rescue those who love me. I will protect those who trust in my name. When they call on me, I will answer; I will be with them in trouble, I will rescue them and honor them. I will satisfy them with a long life and give them my salvation." - Psalm 91

it took for me to travel there be better spent if I just sent it over? After explaining to him my doubts, he answered me honestly, with sincerity and assurance, explaining why I needed to go. I needed to go and see for myself the country, to meet the people, and that me going would mean more than any money being sent. Hearing this spoken from a native of the land, I felt my doubts dissolve and permission being granted to go.

On May 13th, 2015, I finally wrote to Bishop Okabe. I thought it'd take a while to hear from him, if I were to hear from him, but several days later I was surprised with joy. The bishop had written back inviting me to come and visit his ministry. Three months later I boarded a plane that would take me to my destiny that awaited in Uganda.

August 21, 2015

"I am African not because I was born in Africa, but because Africa was born in me." - Kwame Nkrumah

*I'm sitting in my last flight from Nairobi, Kenya to Entebbe, Uganda. I've waited so long for this moment it's hard to not be emotional, but I'm **here**! God brought me **here**. He led me here, for such a time as this.*

Jet-lagged, I stayed my first night in Kampala, Uganda's capital, before traveling by bus the next morning to my final destination. When I arrived to Mbale, I was greeted by the bishop and his wife, and the next day attended their church service. The church was packed because it was their annual

conference with all the church plants coming together and this Sunday a visiting pastor was preaching. Bishop Okabe introduced me to the congregation that morning and shared the story behind me coming after having read one of his books. When the visiting pastor came up to preach, he greeted me from the stage as well and asked if I would join him to pray over the congregation. As he said those words I was so honored, yet humbled. Who was I to do that when the crowd was full of pastors and preachers? I went anyway.

As I stood there, the pastor told me what a good thing it was that I came to visit and what it meant to them. As he spoke those words, much like my friend from the Congo had told me, it really was important that I went for myself. Those years of questioning if I would do more good sending money than going for myself, I knew were all untrue, and that this was what I was always meant to do. It was an overwhelming and beautiful moment that for me, only marked the beginning of my journey.

My first trip to Uganda was all about relationships. There were so many incredible and life-giving moments during that trip I experienced while creating lasting friendships. The school was on holiday so many of the children were back in their villages visiting family, but there were some children and young adults who were still at the orphanage because they had nowhere to go, and these are the ones I spent most of my time with. My first day visiting the orphanage, Vincent, a young man around my age who worked under Bishop Okabe,

and Jackie, a sixteen-year-old girl who lived there as well, gave me a tour of Impact Ministries: the church, classrooms, dormitories, dining hall still being built, the well where they got their water, the place where they washed their clothes, and the courtyard the children played in.

After initially meeting Jackie and discovering we both liked to dance, she and some of the other girls began teaching me choreography from the youth worship team. Dance is a huge part of the culture and it became a routine that I would spend my afternoons dancing with the girls, and then joining in on the youth's dance ministry practices. At the end of my trip, I choreographed a dance for me and some of the girls that we ended up performing at church my last Sunday there.

There were so many moments where I was given the opportunity to speak about dreams and pursuing the passions God places in our hearts whether at a church youth service, or during a radio broadcast for youth, or simply in various conversations with those I met. I remember having a conversation with Pastor Joel, the youth leader, and another pastor and them asking me how I was able to follow my dreams. I acknowledged God's hand in seeing my dreams come to life, and also mentioned that it takes work and action, and being able to do the little things that lead to the big things. During a youth broadcast at Faith Radio, I felt my soul on fire as we discussed the topic of following our dreams and how to actually put a plan to action. In the back of my mind I kept thinking that what I was experiencing in

that moment was it, me living my dreams and fulfilling my God-given calling in life, to not only want to go higher, but to raise others higher. I felt such a privilege to be able to be in Uganda, sharing with my new friends encouragement to not lose heart in their quest to fulfill their God-given calling.

The people that I met both young and old alike, when asked about their dreams for life and the future, many had two things in common. The first was desiring a job that consisted of owning their own business or going to school and furthering their education to get a good job, and the second thing was that everyone I spoke to wanted to serve God in a meaningful way in their lives. What astounded me most while listening in these moments was that there was such a hunger for knowledge and to be educated, yet such a lack of resources to do so. It weighed heavy on my heart.

Knowledge was a word that continuously resounded in my head during my trip. I felt like God was telling me that with more knowledge, I could help more people. And in a country where there was such a hunger to learn, grow and be educated to succeed in life, yet little to no opportunity, I felt like I owed it to those who couldn't go, to go for them and then teach them what I had learned. When I got back to Los Angeles, I applied to grad school and two years later graduated with my MBA, fulfilling what I believed to be a God-given call to truly gain more knowledge to help more people, and specifically to help my brothers and sisters in Uganda.

The hardest thing to deal with during my trip was coming to terms with the standard of living for many people there. Uganda is such a beautiful country and rich in natural resources, but it's also contaminated with corruption that makes it hard for the general population to succeed in life and rise above poverty. My heart broke with each new story I heard and witnessing firsthand the reality of life for many Ugandans. One of the worst part is, I didn't have to go to the slums, the poorest of the poor in Uganda, to be broken by what I saw.

Being at the orphanage alone, though the children are taken care of the best Impact Ministries can afford, if the ministry doesn't have the funds, certain needs can go unmet. I remember being in the dormitories that would never be considered livable by American standards: mud walls, watered-down paint, barely-padded and old mats on worn and rusted bunk beds, not enough mosquito nets for every child, with spiders and insects crawling around in the corners because of unsealed and open windows.

Or the meals that the children received; at times throughout the year if there is famine and food prices increase, the children may only be fed once or twice a day depending on funds available. When I was there, the children were given grits in the morning and posho (grounded-maize cooked into a mashed potato-like consistency) in the afternoon with cooked vegetables if any were available that day, if not, cooked beans. In those moments, I would think of

American children, even my own little nieces and nephews, who were picky eaters, granted, they were able to be given their circumstances. But not here. There are so many details I could describe from what I saw. And I write them not to degrade, but to share and make real for those who do not know of these realities. This is the norm for many.

For over five years, I dedicated my life to work for a leading nonprofit on Skid Row, Los Angeles' designated area for the homeless. The area, known best amongst locals and even state and nationwide as being inhabited by America's poorest of the poor, for me, is nothing compared to what I saw in Uganda. In America, we talk about poverty and the rising homeless population (made up of mostly adults), but over my five years working on Skid Row, knowing and understanding all the accessible resources available to those who are seeking help, it is incomparable. I think the hardest part to accept, and one that I wrestled with often in my heart over the years, is that these are innocent children whose only crime is being born into poverty. They didn't choose this for themselves.

I felt like my first trip in so many ways emptied me and at the same time awakened me. Now that I had seen with my own eyes, I knew, I would never be the same, I could never be the same, and I didn't want to. I reflected on my trip in a confession for my blog:

December 31, 2015

Two weeks. That's all I needed, if that, to confirm where I believed my heart had been these past eight years. Every second there I knew I was exactly where God desired me to be and was living out my God-given dream, what I was created for. I worked with Impact Ministries Uganda, a church that also runs a school and orphanage. My time was spent mostly with the children who called the orphanage home. These hearts, these faces, I will never forget and can't wait to see again. One thing that was a recurring question was when I would be back. My answer was God willing I would be back, though I couldn't promise a time. And so I asked God myself, believing I would be back, when that would be. I received my answer on my journey home.

My initial flight out of Uganda was cancelled due to an engine not working; we were ushered out of the airplane in the middle of the night and escorted to a nearby hotel – checking in through customs to reenter Uganda. Getting to bed at 4:30am, I didn't wake up and get out of bed until late morning. When I did, I spent my first moments with God, thanking Him for everything that had happened during my time in Uganda, and praying for what all was to come, and to show me what to do with all that my eyes had seen.

As I sat in that Ugandan hotel room, basking in the light of the morning and talking to God, I heard Him say, "Look up, for your redemption is here." I do not know what all that means in regard to me or Uganda, all I know is that I had found what I had been anticipating and hoping for, and God gave that to me during my time in Africa.

Redemption was found in Uganda. Redemption, for having chosen victory over defeat in my accident and believing God for a greater destiny than I knew, and redemption that because of my accident, how I was inadvertently given a way to go to Africa.

When I got back home, although there was some culture shock, more than anything it was as mentioned before, an awakening. There I was in a nice apartment, with a nice car and a good job, while my friends in Uganda were just surviving. As I've shared about the period of eight years God used to impress on me of knowing I'd be in Africa one day, I wondered after my trip if those moments would stop since I had fulfilled that call. But they haven't. They have changed, yes, but they're still here. And now, instead of the knowing that I have to go, it's a remembrance of those I left behind, not forgetting them, and a knowing: I know, that I know, that I know, God has called me to help them. The only way then they have changed, is that these impressions now have faces, my friends.

Her Scars Were Beautiful
(Names have been changed to protect the privacy of individuals)

I met Rebecca on my first trip to Uganda. She was a little girl with a scar that spread over her scalp. I was told that her scar came from a reaction to malaria medication. My initial time with her, Rebecca stayed a little behind the group, yet still followed the older girls. When I saw her two

years later she had outgrown her previous shyness and we became friends.

Ruth, I met for the first time in the summer of 2017. She had arrived to the orphanage shortly after I left in August 2015, after having been abused. The scars she bore were great. Her scars came from a reprimand and her abuse served as punishment. And now, the marks she carried showed the severity.

Appalled, devasted, and heartbroken, I was amazed at these little girls' joy and zeal for life; they were best friends and adorable. We laughed, played, and danced together, we talked about things we liked. There was nothing out of the norm for them, and this was their life at all of seven years old. They were perfectly happy and content with who they were and how they were. They were undeniably beautiful.

It put everything into perspective for me, and my only desire was to give them love, encouragement, and speak hope and life into theirs. *Beauty Marks* is dedicated to Ruth and Rebecca because I see a future where they use their own scars to proclaim God's grace and redemption and bring hope and freedom to many. This is my prayer for these little ones, in Jesus' powerful name.

They are Worthy of More

I didn't know when I would be back in Uganda when I came home from my first trip in 2015, but less than two years

later, God allowed me to travel there once more. This next trip was focused on mainly working with the young women at Impact Ministries. Whereas children up to age fifteen are taught at the ministry's school, higher education isn't always available to the older children and young adults. If the ministry has the extra money to put toward their education, they do so, but that isn't always available. And outside of the ministry, it is Ugandan culture in general to elevate men, and women are placed in a secondary role which usually means less opportunity given to them.

When I met with these young women, thirteen in total, I wanted them to see how accessible their dreams really could be when breaking down goals into a plan of action made up of tangible steps. Our purpose was threefold: to discuss their dreams and goals for their lives; then to discern their gifts, talents, and skillsets, and how to use them toward achieving their dreams; and last, to create a life plan of goals to see their dreams fulfilled. For some girls that meant going back to school for higher education, and for others, it meant vocational training, an apprenticeship, or starting their own business with the skillset they already had. Visiting toward the end of my graduate program, it was so fun and useful to teach some of the basics of business I had learned that could be adapted into their lives and career plans.

These were just plans and in theory, doable, yet in practice, could seem so much harder. Most of these girls had nothing of their own and relied on Impact Ministries for

basic necessities. And for those who did work, most of the time it meant they were working just to scrape by. Jobs are scarce in Uganda, and even if you are given the opportunity to go to school for higher education, there is no guarantee of an available position once you've graduated. Work politics are widespread and a matter of who you know. So, we could write out goals and a plan for each individual girl, but there were so many other factors to be considered. There were times I wrestled with helplessness, wondering if what I was doing was actually beneficial or giving the girls a false sense of hope. But my purpose was my resolve.

Given the state and politics of Uganda, there is no guarantee that if these girls further their education they will succeed in a future career. And there is no confident assurance that running their own businesses will grant them a successful future either. Investing in these girls' futures may be supplying them with what they need to grow their own gardens to provide food for themselves, and perhaps sell what is left over. I was impressed by one girl whose current way of making money is going to the flea market to purchase items, then reselling them for a profit.

The truth is, there are unknowns that cannot be answered in the present, but there is hope for the future, faith in God to do the impossible, and a determination of will to see this brought to life and give these girls a fighting chance. I believe in these young women. These girls have grown up in rough conditions and lived through trying and unfavorable

circumstances, I have no doubt they have what it takes to continue to succeed in their lives.

I met with the girls as a group and then individually, hearing their stories and getting to know them for myself. It was such an honor. Meeting after meeting, I was astounded at these young women's hearts that were so full of compassion toward those in need. As my sole purpose was to help them as they had their own needs, they too were thinking of others to help. There wasn't one of them who didn't have the desire to use their life as service to others.

In our personal meetings, one of the questions I asked the girls when discussing talents and skills was if they had ever received an award for anything and most girls never had. At the end of my trip I had the girls come to a lunch gathering where I gave them each an award. I based these awards off my time spent with them and the specific trait that came to me with each one.

All girls had unmistakable qualities that made me believe these traits would carry with them throughout their lives and be of importance. For Babra, it was *kindness*. During both my trips she had always shown such hospitality to me, inviting me to lunch and cooking several times, and I saw the kindness she showed to others as well. For Stella, it was *gentleness*. She had such a gentle spirit, reserved, yet willing to engage with others. Sharon was *strength*. As an Ethiopian refugee, she had left her family to escape her war-torn country. Catherine's word was *beauty*. Since I had

met her in 2015, her presence and stature would cause me to think if she was in America she would surely have a future in modeling. Eve's word was *joyful.* Only in her early 20's, Eve worked to survive while also caring for her late-sister's young children. She seemed to always wear a smile. Joan's word was *playful,* her witty humor made me laugh often during my time getting to know her. And Rachel's word was *composed,* her serene nature proved that. For Jackie, it was *leader.* Over my two years of knowing her, she had become one of my closest Ugandan friends. I saw how she led others and served as a role model to her younger sisters and friends alike. Jane's word was *confidence.* She was such a character, I have no doubt that she can achieve anything she sets her mind too. Eva was the *innovator.* All the ideas and creativity she had, it's endless potential just waiting to be tapped. And Rose was the *storyteller.* She loved to write and wanted to do so in her future. Peace was rightfully so, a *peacemaker.* I hold dear the conversations I've had with her and her desire to keep peace with others and maintain unity. And last was Caroline, who was *faithful.* As I heard her story, I kept seeing parallels to my own. Her story of unwavering faith was inspiring to hear.

These girls all have purpose and their lives have meaning. God could've instilled the desire in me to go to any other country in the world, but He chose Uganda. He could've brought me to any town in Uganda, but He sent me to Mbale. I could've met any other group of girls, but He brought this specific one into my life. There are people all over the world

who are in need and who deserve help, but out of a whole world to choose from, God brought me here. I feel so blessed and so honored to have met these girls and to have spent the time I did with them and I pray for their futures, for God to do mighty things in their lives, and for them to be used greatly by God to touch lives in return.

This time when I left Uganda, I was resolved to write and finish *Beauty Marks* as a way to help my sisters and friends there, and to create a means of support to aid in meeting their needs and the young women growing up at the orphanage who will follow them.

"I love doing preposterous things. I don't know anything more exhilarating and delightful than turning weakness into strength, fear into faith, and that which has been marred into perfection. That is my special work. Transforming things – to transform her into – well, we shall see what she finds herself transformed into."

- *Hinds Feet on High Places*, Hannah Hurnard

IV

Beauty for Ashes

"To all who mourn... he will give beauty for ashes, joy instead of mourning, praise instead of despair."

- Isaiah 61:3

When I woke up on Friday, April 12th, 2013, I didn't know what the day would hold, but I could never have guessed it would include the reality of what it brought. I couldn't foresee that night and the horrible events to take place. I didn't know at the time that there would be an in between state for trauma, that though my accident happened in a moment, there would be six months of physical healing and recovery to follow with days of frustration, irritation, and wishing to be anywhere besides where I was. I didn't know then that my body would in some ways be permanently affected, or that I would have to make a choice to allow that night to permanently affect me emotionally and mentally or choose to give it to God and allow for Him to heal me inwardly as well. I could not have known of the darkness to come that would surround me that night.

What I did wake up knowing that Friday morning was the role of a good God in my life. That I had been created in His image and purposed for greatness that would fulfill my life and give honor to Him. I had been made to love and give love, to live with all my might, and walk in remembrance of God's love and faithfulness to me throughout my life. I knew before the day started that God was with me and would be with me in every moment that was to come my way. I knew that nothing was going to happen that day that God wouldn't first allow in my life. I woke up that morning knowing that in whatever I faced, no matter what, God was

bigger than my circumstances and had the power to use them for good in my life.

Six months after my accident, I didn't know I would be given my first opportunity to travel for With All Her Might, or that in the years to follow, God would bring some unbelievable and thrilling opportunities for me to travel and do ministry. I didn't know it would include traveling to Africa so soon, or that God would send me specifically to Uganda. I could never have guessed the people I would meet and the imprint they would leave in my heart forever, or the conviction I felt of knowing where God wanted me and whom I was called to help.

That Friday morning, I didn't know just how much faith and courage I would have to willfully activate in my life, with God's help, to defeat fear and doubt while overcoming obstacles in my way. I didn't know in that moment I would be given wounds for God to heal, and that He'd give beauty to my scars, and bring redemption not only to me, but to others. That by one act of vulnerability, there would be the potential to affect and change hearts and lives around the world.

I didn't know any of that at the time, but I see now. Reflecting on everything I have experienced in my life since the accident, it was all worth it. A part of me will probably always wish my accident never happened, but at the same time, I can see how God clearly used it for something wonderful. He was working behind the scenes all along

and He truly did have a greater purpose for it than I could possibly have known in the moment.

I am in awe of what He has done in my life evidenced by His grace, beauty, and redemption for my scars. He gave me beauty for ashes.

Beauty Marks is my testament to that.

AFTERWORD

If you have purchased this book, then you have touched
the lives of my friends back in Uganda. All profits made
through *Beauty Marks* are designated to help these young
women to craft their skills, afford a higher education, and
become self-sustainable and attain a better life. It is my hope
that this will be a continuous flow of aid to help each new
generation being raised at Impact Ministries. Funds will also
be directed to improving the quality of life for the children
who live at the orphanage and attend school there. May
God multiply what is given so that our brothers and sisters
in Uganda will be overwhelmed by an unending outpouring
of blessings.

Do you have the desire to share your own story with the
world about how God has healed and used your scars? *Beauty
Marks* is not finished, for it is a continuing story, and I would
be honored to have the privilege to write and share yours.
The book's original intent was to be a compilation of stories
from women – and still will be. If you would like to share
your own Beauty Mark and use your story to touch the lives

of others, please write to me at staci@withallhermight.com to be considered. All profits will be used to fund continuous efforts in Uganda. May God bless you for your willing vulnerability, and may He use your scars to reach others and change the world.

For more information, visit www.withallhermight.com

For more information on Impact Ministries Uganda,

visit www.impactministriesuganda.com.

CPSIA information can be obtained
at www.ICGtesting.com
Printed in the USA
BVHW030550220319
543335BV00022B/6/P

9 781973 655091